Slash Your Operating Budget!

Five Secrets to

Recovering Wasted Budget Dollars

By David Cantliffe

Printed in the United States of America

First Printing, 2014

ISBN-13: 978-06922006-6-7

ISBN-10: 0692200665

Published by David Cantliffe
www.SlashYourOperatingBudget.com

Edited by Jennifer-Crystal Johnson
www.JenniferCrystalJohnson.com

Book cover art by Mala Baranove
asfaigraphics@yahoo.com

Cover design and formatting by Jennifer-Crystal Johnson
www.JenniferCrystalJohnson.com

This book is dedicated to my parents, who taught me through example the rewards of focus and consistent effort.

And to my amazing daughters, who continue to remind me how blessed I am to be their dad as well as their cheerleader and guide. I continue to learn from and be inspired by them.

Table of Contents

FOREWORD

Hidden (Hard Dollar) Cost Savings in My Operating Budget? ... I Didn't Believe it Until I Saw it Firsthand

By Eric Newman

My name is Eric Newman, corporate controller for Saddle Creek Logistics Services and a client of the author.

While still a family-owned company, Saddle Creek has grown to be a leading third-party provider offering comprehensive integrated logistics services. Just like our founders, today's associates are committed to doing, *"Whatever It Takes!"* to ensure the complete satisfaction of our customers.

Saddle Creek Logistics Services has been recognized by *Inc.* magazine as one of the fastest-growing private companies in America. Based in Lakeland, FL, Saddle Creek has grown significantly and now employs more than 2,200 associates and operates more than 16 million square feet of space in 37 locations nationwide.

The author of this book, David Cantliffe, asked me to provide insights for readers of this guide to recovering hidden costs. Although this book addresses corporate expense categories in general, I thought the easiest way to provide insight is to share my personal experiences while working with David's company, BottomLine Advantage LLC.

Like most successful businesses, our focus is on making sure that we exceed our customers' expectations. We employ competent and motivated associates to acquire the needed resources and materials in order to provide exceptional results for our clients.

As Saddle Creek itself offers specialized logistics services, I'm already aware that no person or business can be experts in all areas. When several additional expense categories were recently added to my oversight responsibilities, I wondered if Saddle Creek had savings potential within them.

We occasionally use outsourced experts to help us in specific areas and one of them introduced David to me. His company specializes in an expense category that we wanted to review.

First, I was happy to find out that their business model was contingency based. No up-front costs and they delivered results which we got to approve before any fee was owed. And the project fee could be paid over three years without interest so we could eliminate out-of-pocket costs.

This approach definitely appeased my concern about our risk or having to go through a budget approval process.

Next, David outlined their process and reviewed how each step was preceded by a guaranteed outcome before starting that step. We knew what our outcome would be before investing any time.

David shared with us that he guaranteed we had at least $227,325 net hard dollar *savings potential* based on our company's annual revenues that exceed $100 million and our equipment fleet which exceeds 15 devices.

If that hard dollar savings potential wasn't confirmed, BottomLine Advantage would donate $1,000 to our favorite charity. I was definitely curious to see if it we did indeed have that much savings potential.

We simply provided some current invoices and BottomLine Advantage analyzed them to confirm our savings potential would exceed $227,325 hard dollars.

I should point out that BottomLine Advantage offers two guarantees that, at first glance, look similar.

The first, a Savings Potential Guarantee, is to confirm that companies with annual revenues exceeding $100 million and who have more than 15 devices will have at least $227,325 net hard dollar savings or recovery potential. It's basically their tool to break through the typical natural reaction of, "we're already handled," "not interested," etc.

The second is the Project Savings Guarantee. This can be equal to or greater than $227,325. This demonstrates BottomLine Advantage's confidence in their process and skill because if they miss or deliver just at the Project Savings Guarantee they complete the project and waive any fee.

That's many labor hours invested on their part and we're the sole beneficiary. I think that's called risk reversal in our favor.

In our case, they *guaranteed* they'd recover at least $227,325 net to us, in writing, within our agreement.

As I just mentioned, their penalty for non-performance would be completing the entire cost recovery project at no charge and we'd keep all the savings that were generated.

As you can imagine, I was confident that we had no risk.

During the project, we stayed in control of all milestone decisions, had minimal time invested, and saw significant cost reduction as well as improvements to our vendor support commitments.

I also gained valuable insight into this industry's inner workings, which I know will be helpful during all future renegotiations.

As an aside, BottomLine's policy is to donate $1,000 to our favorite charity after successfully exceeding their Project Savings Guarantee. So our favorite charity will now receive a $1,000 donation as well.

The project was implemented as outlined and on schedule. I'm happy to report that the net savings BottomLine Advantage generated exceeded their Project Savings Guarantee.

Even if we had wanted to complete a potential vendor review internally, I now realize that without the extensive industry knowledge and experience that BottomLine Advantage has, our results would have been inferior in comparison.

It kind of seems like we've found free operating capital. BottomLine Advantage secured better pricing and improved vendor support with very little of our time or effort.

I'm convinced we wouldn't have come close to their results and we get to pay BottomLine Advantage over three years with budget dollars previously being sent to a vendor while keeping the lion's share ourselves.

In hindsight, the only reason that I wouldn't have used BottomLine Advantage is if I felt we could have produced similar or superior results internally.

I realize now that the best way to test that premise is to get a written commitment from your procurement team as to what they *guarantee* they'll generate. Then let BottomLine Advantage review it to determine if they'll guarantee *at least* the same amount.

If they do, basically they've confirmed they'll deliver at least what your internal team has guaranteed for free (BottomLine Advantage has to exceed the guarantee figure to benefit).

And this frees up my internal team to focus on other key initiatives. So I get double the results for the same cost.

My experience working with BottomLine Advantage has been a classic win-win scenario for Saddle Creek Logistics Services. I look forward to leveraging the knowledge and experience of additional contingency/performance based experts from their consortium of Expense Category Experts.

Preface

Why Reading this Book *Will* Increase Your Operating Capital and Profits

"Don't worry about people stealing your ideas. If your ideas are any good, you'll have to ram them down people's throats."

– Howard Aiken

Many experts say that the business landscape is more competitive than it's ever been. While I agree that the pace of business is faster than ever before, I feel the world of business has always been competitive.

Being on the front line attracting new clients for over 33 years, I haven't seen any appreciable change in the intensity of competition. However, my understanding of how to receive the best value from your vendors has changed dramatically.

First, let me comment on the term "best value." I've found that "best value" is defined differently within each organization. Basically, it's your organization's optimal mix of pricing and vendor support. There is no "one size fits all."

Having been both a vendor (over 25 years) and client advocate (over eight years), I've learned first-hand that by *only* using standard cost management techniques, organizations of all types and sizes are overpaying their vendors by millions of hard budget dollars.

This book was written to highlight the fact that you can make quantum improvements in your operating efficiency (read significantly lower hard dollar costs) while simultaneously improving vendor support in most expense categories.

The "catch" is that you can't achieve quantum improvements utilizing standard cost/vendor support management practices. Of course, some improvement can always be achieved... just not quantum improvements.

This concise guide is intended to provide a template you can use to redeploy precious hard budget dollars currently being overpaid to (many of your) vendors.

Whether you have stalled infrastructure upgrade initiatives, new product development, or market expansion needs, you'll free up capital to implement these projects. If done right, you'll experience improved vendor relationships and support as well.

Of course, the choice of what to do with your freed-up capital is up to you. Whether you reinvest in your business or simply drop it to your bottom line, ultimately it will increase your profits.

Chapter One

Your Company *Does* Have Hard Dollar Recovery Potential

"Nothing is a waste of time if you use the experience wisely."

– Rodin

Your company *does* have hard dollar recovery potential. How do I know that?

The answer comes by way of a question: How is your company managing its spend categories now?

If it's like most companies, it's by benchmarking current costs, requesting bids from three vendors and comparing their responses with your current costs, and possibly the costs of peer-sized companies.

Here's the weakness of this traditional approach: Although you can determine what vendors are currently offering and measure incremental changes from your current costs, *you still don't know what's possible.*

Secret #1: Traditional vendor price comparisons don't produce the best value for your company.

To receive the best possible value (your optimal mix of lowest pricing and best possible vendor support), you must have deep insight into the industry that is serving that particular business need.

In order to leverage deep insight into an industry, your organization can either hire industry experts full time for each of your key expense categories and cross-train them for additional roles, or you can "lease" one, and if done correctly, at no out-of-pocket cost.

Business executives immediately recognize that it's cost prohibitive to hire full time experts for each of their critical or large expense categories. Most of the time, the solution adopted is hiring a procurement or supply management department manager who then manages all the expense categories for the company.

The problem is that you need experts in each significant expense category or you'll end up *considerably* overpaying your vendors and receiving inferior support as well. From experience, for my clients that are over $100 million in annual revenue, "considerably overpaying" means by *hundreds of thousands to millions* of hard budget dollars.

An Expense Category Expert (ECE) is defined as a person that has had extensive experience within a specific industry. I'll define "extensive" as having been in an executive management position for at least five years within their industry. This probably means they'll have something like 10-15 years of experience within the industry.

After investing 18 years (as a sales person for a vendor) within my own industry, I found out firsthand that, until you are in an executive management position, there's a lot that you don't know that you don't know about your industry. More about that later.

Switching gears for a moment, I'd like to tell you a story that highlights the importance of engaging the right expert.

I moved to Colorado over 30 years ago to attend CU's (University of Colorado) MBA program and because skiing is one of my passions. I've taught all my daughters to ski and we escape to the mountains during winter weekends and school vacations. Last February we were playing in about a foot of fresh powder from an overnight storm. It was a beautiful ski day, still snowing and in the mid 20's.

My 13-year-old daughter was just starting to get the hang of carving (ski lingo for a crisp, non-sliding turn) and was making some beautiful turns. Because she was just getting the hang of this new skill, she was not initiating turns as fluidly or quickly as is needed in fresh powder.

One of her skis got hung up in the snow and she went down hard, face first. Unfortunately her bindings didn't release and her left knee got really twisted.

It was an abrupt end to an amazing powder day.

After making sure she was OK and getting her skis back on, she was able to ski to the bottom. Fortunately we were staying at a lodge right at the slope. I got her back inside and assessed her condition to determine if we were making an immediate visit to the emergency room.

Luckily there didn't seem to be significant damage, but I could see she was in pain. We started icing her knee, kept it elevated, and had her stay off of it as much as possible. That night she convinced me she would be fine and wanted to stay in the mountains until our planned checkout day.

When we got back home a couple of days later (on a Sunday), she was still hurting so we went to our local emergency room. The ER doctor examined her knee thoroughly and took an X-ray. He confirmed there was no major damage and her ACL was intact.

He gave us a temporary pain mitigation routine. Although this ER physician had personally invested at least 11 years in his career path to become a doctor, he told us that, for a thorough evaluation of my daughter's knee, we would need to see a sports-focused orthopedic specialist. We got a referral from the ER doctor and made an appointment for the following week.

The orthopedic specialist examined my daughter's knee and ordered an MRI to determine if there were any tears or damage to her knee. After the he analyzed the MRI, the good news was there was no significant damage to her knee.

He gave us a very specific healing regime that included anti-inflammatories, exercises, and stretches. After following his advice to the T, a number of weeks later my daughter's knee was healed.

> "The only source of knowledge is experience."
> – Albert Einstein

This got me thinking about the similarities and differences between the medical and business communities.

The ER physician, like the general (or family) practitioner, is trained to know a little about a lot of organs and systems within the human body. This is similar to the procurement or supply management function within a business. Procurement or supply management must acquire hundreds (sometimes thousands) of items to keep a business operating healthily.

What's different is that the medical community has readily adopted the practice of referring patients to doctors who focus on a specific system within the human body. I've rarely seen procurement or supply management teams seek help from expense category experts.

Medical professionals spend four years at an undergraduate college, four more years at medical school, and then at least one more year as a medical resident. Even with nine years of study and application, it takes an additional one to five years to become a specialist (expert) within a specific human body function or system. Then the specialist focuses only on their specialty to provide the best results possible.

The health care industry has decided that a doctor can't be an expert in all facets of the human body. Their protocol seems to be to have a general practitioner (or ER physician) determine if a health issue can be clearly identified and solved. If not, they decide what specialty and specialist to refer the patient to.

As reported by Gary Keller and Jay Papasan in *The One Thing*:

> In 1993, psychologist K. Anders Ericsson published "The Role of Deliberate Practice in the Acquisition of Expert Performance" in the journal *Psychological Review*. As a benchmark for understanding mastery, this article debunked the idea that an expert performer was *gifted,* a *natural,* or even a *prodigy.* Ericsson essentially gave us our first real insights into mastery and birthed the idea of the "10,000-hour rule." His research identifies a common pattern of regular and deliberate practice over the course of years in elite performers that made them what they were – elite.

To receive the absolute best value (your optimal mix of lowest pricing and best possible vendor support) from your vendor, you must intimately know the industry you're evaluating. This includes understanding the vendor's motivators, how those motivators change throughout the calendar year, and how to "repackage" your account to present it to vendors in a way that appeals to those motivators. By speaking the industry's internal language and knowing their cost of goods benchmarks as well as the true cost of differing levels of customer support, you will always receive the best value possible from that industry's vendors.

By communicating with the industry in their own language, you can craft your message (requests for bids, service level agreements, etc.) in a way that positions you as "one of them."

If you understand the vendor's motivators, you can present your account and requests in a way to create a mutual win. This appears counterintuitive because most people think that customers and clients always have directly opposing goals (customer wants to receive the lowest price while the vendor wants to achieve the highest price/profit margin). Not so, once you know and understand the vendor's motivators.

Understanding that expense category's cost of goods benchmarks allows you to determine if the results of your formal bid are the best possible rather than just what vendors are offering at that time. By knowing vendor costs for varying levels of customer support, you can judge if what vendors are offering can be improved.

Using a travel analogy, I lived in Maui, Hawaii for two years after graduating from college. After several months I began to meet people who had grown up on Maui and others who had lived there for many years.

I found that locals always had the inside track, usually by knowing the most beautiful places on the island, the best restaurants and lowest prices for groceries, etc. Insider information was only shared freely within the "local" community.

If you can appear like a "local" within you vendor's industry, you'll always be treated better. That's where an expense category expert comes in handy. They have spent more than five years in executive management within the industry (which usually means 10-15 years total) and are intimately familiar with all the language, nuances, and motivators of industry vendors. They are seen by vendors as a "local."

They know cost of goods benchmarks, what levels of support vendors can offer, and whether you are receiving the best possible value (your optimal mix of lowest pricing and best possible vendor support).

From my experience, the best expense category experts employ a performance-based business model. They are confident in their ability to produce results for clients. They'll guarantee their results on the front end and never charge any up-front fees.

This risk reversal eliminates the possibility of having your time wasted and/or paying for something that you don't receive. Only after exceeding their written, hard dollar performance guarantee will the expense category expert receive any compensation.

Even better, their fee is paid from the savings previously being overpaid to one of your vendors.

Please note that, although I mostly mention cost savings, I am assuming that *quality benchmarks* are being evaluated as well. Cost savings are only valuable if the level of quality for equipment and/or services and the vendor support being provided are at least equal (preferably enhanced) to what your company has been receiving.

There should always be a front end benchmark process on the quality aspects of your vendor experience as well as the cost benchmarks. The quality benchmarks must be measureable to enable your company to identify any potential improvements along with cost reduction.

All competent ECEs can provide a benchmarking template to ensure efficient measurement of changes in quality.

Secret #2: You company does have hard dollar recovery potential.

Chapter 1 Takeaways

Is your company still using the traditional marketplace evaluation of getting pricing from three vendors?

You may reduce your current costs, but you still won't know what pricing and support options are possible.

An industry expert is required to determine the best possible value in that respective industry. You can hire one full time or "lease" one in the form of an Expense Category Expert (ECE).

For quite some time, the medical profession has recognized the importance and correct use of both the general practitioner and the specialist.

A specialist or category expert has insight and experience within their area of expertise that's far beyond that of a "general practitioner," regardless of whether it's in business, medicine, technology, etc.

Psychologist K. Anders Ericsson's research gave us the first real insights that mastery of a subject requires 10,000 hours of deliberate practice. If a subject is studied exclusively for eight hours per day, five days per week, it will take 4.7 years to attain mastery. If a subject is studied just two hours per day, five days per week, it will take 18.9 years to attain mastery.

Achieving hard dollar cost savings doesn't mean you must sacrifice the quality of products, services, or vendor support.

Chapter Gifts

You can download a spreadsheet template summarizing the hard dollar value of your internal team's cost reduction targets listed as resource document #1, "The hard dollar value of my internal team's cost reduction targets," at:

www.slashyouroperatingbudget.com/resources

You can download a savings potential checklist listed as resource document #2, "Savings potential checklist," at:

www.slashyouroperatingbudget.com/resources

Chapter Two

Why is This Important to Me?

"It ain't what you don't know that gets you into trouble.
It's what you know for sure that just ain't so."

— Mark Twain

Even though prospective clients are consistently skeptical about having *any* significant hard dollar savings potential, let's assume for a moment that it's true. The next question is: Why is this even important to you?

My company's target clients typically range from $100 million to $5 billion in annual revenue. We know from our experience that 89% of the time we identify and recover at least $227,325 hard dollars. Sometimes it's in the millions. *This happens even when our prospective client is <u>absolutely sure</u> that they have zero savings potential.*

Naturally, savings potential will vary with different expense categories as well as by the size of your company. Since we've documented our results, let's use what we collected over the last eight years to explore if this is important to you.

Once clients have confirmed the hard dollars we've recovered for them, they've shared the following uses for their newfound budget dollars.

It's a plethora of budget-stalled initiatives including:

- Desperately needed IT and telecommunications upgrades
- Hiring to address multiple labor needs
- Research and development for new products
- Expanding into new markets
- Marketing
- Advertising
- Leasing additional office space
- Upgrading manufacturing equipment
- Buying needed inventory
- Employee recognition events
- Client appreciation events

- Business travel
- Enhance employee health benefits
- Employee educational benefits

Other benefits clients have shared with us:

- Paying off debt
- Testing the state of their operating efficiency
- Increasing profit

To summarize the many conversations we've had after savings projects with clients, it boils down to having additional working capital to help them achieve their goals faster.

Although every company's recovery results will differ, leveraging performance-based expense category experts will ensure that you maximize working capital to accelerate your goal achievement.

Chapter 2 Takeaways

From my experience, your company has an 89% probability of having a hard dollar cost savings potential of at least $227,325.

What are your currently stalled initiatives?

Would it help your company's growth and/or profitability to fund one or more of your stuck initiatives?

Chapter Gifts

You can download a spreadsheet to quickly outline your budget stalled initiatives, their cost, and their benefit to your company listed as resource document #3, "Budget stalled initiatives," at:

www.slashyouroperatingbudget.com/resources

You can download a checklist to evaluate when each of your expense categories were last reviewed and by whom listed as resource document #4, "When were our expense categories last reviewed? Lists all major expense categories," at:

www.slashyouroperatingbudget.com/resources

Chapter Three

Why Should I Listen to You?

"Ignorance is the beginning of knowledge; knowledge is the
beginning of wisdom; wisdom is the awareness of ignorance."

– William Rotsler

After analyzing current cost benchmarks for hundreds of companies, we know that 89% of the time, we'll recover *at least* $227,325 hard dollars from your operating budget. Budget dollars that you don't realize you're overpaying to vendors. Sometimes the recovery is in the millions.

Because our expertise and track record prove that we're in the trenches daily, we know the territory. Because we're confident enough in our abilities, if we don't meet or exceed our cost recovery guarantee (which is at least $227,325 hard dollars), we'll waive our fee. I hope you agree that this demonstrates confidence in our experience and abilities.

We've saved clients over $15.9 million hard budget dollars so far and have the testimonials to back it up.

I've personally invested over 33 years in the industry I serve, yet I know from experience that my credentials are of limited interest to you. More important is how these ideas will help you to identify any risk.

To accomplish that, I'd like to tell you a story about my own transition from sales rep to dealership principal and the shocking discovery I made.

In my industry, salespeople are typically paid a percentage of the gross profit for hardware installs. Two important data points are the selling price and cost of goods.

For most of my 18-year selling career, the sales force was told that the employer's cost of goods was being marked up by a percentage to cover overhead expenses. Sounded fair enough to me. Commissions were calculated from difference of the "packed" (marked up) cost of goods and the selling price (or funded amount if leased).

When I transitioned to becoming a dealer principal, it was the first time in my career that I was personally involved in purchase of equipment and consumables. What I discovered was that the cost of goods for equipment and consumables were significantly lower than what I had been previously told. In addition, there were several manufacturer quota-based rebates and bonuses that made the "true" cost of goods even lower.

I immediately understood that vendors in my industry earned a lot more margin than I was led to believe. I realized that we could sell and support equipment for less than the standard industry pricing levels and still be profitable.

Although I tucked this thought away at the time, it slowly germinated and was the basic premise upon which my current cost reduction company was founded.

I was very fortunate that several of our first cost reduction clients turned out be important business mentors as well. They helped us understand the critical importance of risk reversal to minimize the skepticism barrier.

They explained that business executives have heard just about every claim and many of those were unfulfilled. Skepticism is understandably strong.

One mentor was Chuck Ochsner, owner of RE/MAX Alliance, the largest RE/MAX franchise in the world. He told me his real estate compensation perspective was, "Deliver results first. Then you've earned your fee."

Ray Seabrook, then-CFO of Ball Corporation (#297 on the 2012 Fortune 500 list at $8.63 billion in annual revenue), told me, "To be attractive to business executives you need to solve a problem and do so without any up-front costs or risk on their part."

I immensely appreciate their advice and the role it played in shaping our business model. Minimizing risk, and with it skepticism, has been a key to my company's growth.

How does all this affect you?

If you have the responsibility to operate your company as efficiently as possible, I'll be revealing secrets that will help you.

Combining the experiences as a vendor with those as an expense category expert whose focus is lowering costs, I know where to find cost savings opportunities.

My goal is to provide you with a roadmap to find your cost reduction opportunities within your own operating budget.

"There is an enormous number of managers who have retired on the job."

– Peter Drucker

Chapter 3 Takeaways

After analyzing hundreds of companies' current costs, we know that your hard dollar cost savings potential is at least $227,325 (and that's in just one expense category).

Transitioning from employee to distributor principal in my industry allowed me to determine firsthand what the *true* costs of goods were for equipment and support.

I was surprised when I learned about the industry's true profit margins (they were much higher than I was led to believe) and realized an efficiently run distributorship could be profitable with lower margins.

Chapter Gifts

You can download the Savings Commitment certificate we use for our target-sized prospective clients to demonstrate that our experience confirms your company has at least $227,325 hard dollar savings potential listed as resource document #5, "Savings Commitment template," at:

www.slashyouroperatingbudget.com/resources

Chapter Four

Untested Skepticism is Costing You Hundreds of Thousands (or More) in Profit

"Those who have trusted where they ought not will surely mistrust where they ought not."

– Marie von Ebner-Eschenbach

Skepticism...

Anyone past kindergarten has had numerous experiences of being taken advantage of and hearing promises made but not kept.

Skepticism is our instinctual defense that grows stronger over time to protect our best interests.

It's one of the two objections we experience that keep prospective clients from maximizing the value that they receive from their vendors. From previous experiences, they perceive they're heading toward a dead end, empty-handed... again! (The other objection is fear-based.)

Usually, skepticism is expressed by executive management while we hear fear-based objections from team members who manage the spend category.

First I'll list many of the objections we've heard when talking with prospective clients that fall into the category of skepticism.

- I don't have the time.
- I'm not interested.
- I already have this handled.
- I don't believe you can really help my company lower its costs.
- We can do this internally just as well as you can.
- I don't want to pay you to accomplish the same thing my team can do.
- Last time I tried this it was a complete waste of my team's time and mine.
- I don't think you'll deliver on your performance guarantee.
- We don't outsource.

- We can do this internally without any cost.
- We just renegotiated with our vendor.

I'm not suggesting that you completely turn off your skepticism. However, I am suggesting that you use the following filter to evaluate offers and claims so you don't dismiss something that will actually help your organization.

Here are some filtering questions to ask yourself:

- Is the ECE asking for any up-front fees? If the ECE is willing to accept all risk of delivering results without any up-front fee, this demonstrates confidence in their expertise and ability to deliver.
- Is the ECE providing a written performance guarantee? A written performance guarantee provided up-front identifies your benefit before you invest your organization's time with the process. Combined with zero up-front fees, you have eliminated your risk (with the exception of the time that it takes to assemble the current cost information on the front end) as well as knowing your minimum savings target before you start.
- Is the ECE willing to be paid their earned fee over time so you can ensure the value that you've received? If the ECE is willing to be paid over time, this is further assurance that the hard dollar savings estimated at project completion are real and can be confirmed over the time period the ECE is compensated.

Fear...

A VP of Procurement shared this recently: he, "will not even consider any assessment or conversation, not another word about (the expense category we were discussing). I'm tired of the BS and I have the best deal. I don't care how much you saved any other organization. They probably are not buying well like I do."

When we speak to team members that are closer to the actual management of the expense category, we experience a shift from skepticism to fear. The fear is rarely addressed directly but rather is expressed in deflecting comments or resistance to truly evaluating a cost reduction opportunity... like the above quote.

Fear-based concerns have numerous variations, but they basically boil down to these two:

- "I'm afraid of what you'll uncover because I'll look incompetent."
- "This is what I do; are you trying to take over this area of my responsibility?"

We've found fear to be the most difficult adversary because it appears to us that the people expressing fear envision that they are protecting their life as they know it.

From the few people that have opened up a little after we worked with their company (after they realized none of their fears materialized and even admitted to learning something from our process), we've heard that they projected being ridiculed after savings were recovered. They continued their doomsday visualization with being fired, their spouse leaving them, and losing their family.

At least it makes more sense why we experience such intense deflecting tactics from expense category managers. They see themselves as fighting for their life!

Admittedly, fear is most often not rational and a very difficult emotion to harness. There are, however, several suggestions we offer.

From personal experience, an ECE is not on a campaign to embarrass or replace any expense category manager. An ECE simply has specialized knowledge in a niche area and can deliver an exceptional result within that niche, similar to a medical specialist.

Expense category managers that have observed our process all report learning industry nuances that they'll apply to other cost reduction projects in the future. After observing our process, they report being more open to new information and processes. The most effective say they will leverage what they learned within their own organization.

We've found that executive management plays a huge role in eliminating fear and resistance by simply giving expense category managers "permission" to further lower their costs without fear of any negative repercussions for not finding it on their own or sooner. There's a permission form you may copy and use at the end of Chapter 10.

This may sound absurd, but without executive management's assurance, there will be resistance to an expense category review.

Let me tie this back to a basic question... Why should I believe you?

The ECE has more at stake than you do. If your cost information is organized, it shouldn't take more than a half hour to provide the needed data. By the way, insist on mutually approving a non-disclosure agreement before providing any current cost information.

It will take the ECE multiple hours to analyze your information. A competent ECE will always complete the analysis at no charge to you. If there isn't sufficient potential hard dollar savings or you decide not to move forward, the ECE isn't compensated for their expense category review.

After analyzing all perspectives of your risk versus an ECE's risk, I believe your risk to be minimal.

Your only risk is the time it takes to provide the initial basic cost information. At that point, the ECE should clearly outline the guaranteed outcome for future steps requiring your time. If they don't, you're using the wrong ECE.

You'll know up-front what your benefits are and the ECE has to deliver on their commitments before they're rewarded.

If you engage an ECE and they don't meet or exceed their performance guarantee, you keep all the hard dollar savings they generate as well as any vendor support improvements. Because they didn't exceed their guarantee, they have not earned any fee.

This is risk reversal (in your favor) at its best.

As I researched quotes and quips for this book, I found a number of "regrettable quotes" that seem to confirm what Mark Twain states at the beginning of Chapter Two. I've included them to help with your daily chuckle....

Regrettable Quotes

"Everything that can be invented has been invented."
Charles H. Duell, Office of Patents, 1899

"We don't like their sound. Groups of guitars are on the way out."
Decca Executive, 1962, after turning down the Beatles

"With over 50 foreign cars already on sale here, the Japanese auto industry isn't likely to carve out a big slice of the US market."
Business Week, August 2, 1968

"There is no reason anyone would want a computer in their home."
Ken Olson, president of Digital Equipment Corp. 1977

"This telephone' has too many shortcomings to be seriously considered as a means of communication."
Western Union, memo, 1876

"Who wants to hear actors talk?"
H.M. Warner, Warner Brothers, 1927

Chapter 4 Takeaways

Skepticism is our instinctual defense that grows stronger over time to protect our best interests.

Skepticism is usually expressed by executives while fear-based objections are more often expressed by expense category managers.

Executive management plays an important role in minimizing the fear of expense category managers by giving the mangers "permission" to explore all options to reduce costs (while maintaining or improving quality and support), including the use of ECE's.

A competent ECE will reverse any perceived risk by evaluating hard dollar savings potential at no charge. The best ECE's will then guarantee a minimum result if you allow them to recover the hard dollar savings they identified. You'll know your worst case outcome before proceeding.

Chapter Gifts

You can download the Project Savings Guarantee that's included as part of my company's ECE agreement. This section of the agreement lists your guaranteed, minimum net hard dollar savings when working with my company. It's a mutually generated figure and makes it easy to know up-front your return for any time invested as well as whether using an ECE is your best option. It's listed as resource document #6, "Project Savings Guarantee," and is located at:

www.slashyouroperatingbudget.com/resources

Chapter Five

Should I Let My Internal Team Handle This?

"Focus is a matter of deciding what things you're not going to do."

– John Carmack

How do you evaluate whether your internal team or an ECE will deliver the best results in a specific expense category? Here "results" is being defined as *your* best mix of lowest cost and best possible vendor support/performance.

First, decide how you'll define and measure the results you desire for a cost reduction effort. Next, evaluate who you think will deliver the best results based on your criteria. The following sub-headings cover things to consider.

Consequence

Competent expense category experts will provide a written guarantee stating the minimum result (hard dollar savings and quality/support metrics) they'll provide up-front.

In our company's case, if we were to just meet our guarantee, we would forfeit any project fee because we must *exceed* the guarantee to earn it (which means you will most likely achieve even greater savings than were guaranteed). At the very least you should know your worst case result before investing any time or effort with an ECE.

Ask your internal team for a written, hard dollar figure that they'll commit to delivering in the same expense category. While it's easy to compare the two figures, you'll also need to determine what their penalty is for non-performance.

If the internal team's penalty for non-performance is something like, "whoops, sorry we missed the target," you should weigh the ECE's consequence significantly higher. For the ECE, missing the target (or even just meeting it) means forfeiting their fee after having invested many hours (it can be hundreds) into a project.

That's a huge consequence difference!

Opportunity Cost

What other projects are top priority for your internal team? Can your team work on other expense categories just as important (or maybe more important) while the ECE focuses on another? I refer to this as your opportunity cost.

One of my clients recently commented that his biggest challenge was a time limitation. He prioritized potential returns for different expense categories. He directed is department to work on the ones with the greatest value to his organization first.

Because no company has unlimited labor resources there were always expense categories that couldn't be focused on. Every month that your company pays more than it needs to for any expense category, you're losing operating capital forever.

For instance, I once worked with a company whose hard dollar savings were $655,387.08 over a three-year period. Every month their team let this expense category remain status quo, they were wasting another $18,205.20 in operating capital.

Even though the $18,205.20 monthly overpayment wasn't crippling in relation to their revenue and cash flow, what other productive uses could they find for this operating capital? I've already mentioned some possibilities in Chapter Two.

This company knew this particular expense category probably had cost reduction potential, but lacked the labor resources to tackle its review.

By leveraging an ECE they stayed focused on their top priorities and recovered additional operating capital to use to benefit their business.

On top of that, there's the question of whether they could have even delivered the same results internally.

Experience

Compare the experience of the ECE and your internal team. Determine whether your internal team has any specialized knowledge or experience within the expense category you are evaluating. This does not give credit for merely managing the expense category. Ask or find out what direct industry experience from the vendor perspective your team has.

How likely is it that your internal team knows the vendor motivators, how those motivators change throughout the calendar year, the vendors' cost of goods benchmarks, and the vendors' cost of providing varying levels of customer support?

Check testimonials from the ECE's clients and, if desired, ask to speak with several of them. You're looking for confirmation that the ECE being considered does or doesn't have the skill and track record to deliver on their promises and commitments. If you determine that they will deliver, do their guarantees top your internal team's commitment?

The Math

- Your internal team's savings commitment.
- List their penalty for not delivering (how real is this commitment?).
- Subtract the labor hours estimated for completion including all team members involved (procurement/supply management, IT, any department heads) times their associated fully-burdened hourly labor cost.

- Subtract your estimate of the cost of delaying other projects your internal team can't be working on because they're focused on this particular expense category.
- This equals your net benefit of cost savings in this expense category for your internal team.

Compare this to:

- ECE's performance/savings guarantee. This is the minimum amount of savings that will be delivered. For my company, this savings amount would have no chargeable fee. We have to *exceed* the savings guarantee to earn any fee. So realize that your actual savings will be higher, but for this exercise you can use the "guarantee" figure.
- Review the penalty for not meeting the savings guarantee. Usually you get to keep all the savings generated and the ECE waives their project fee.
- Subtract the ECE's estimated time commitment for your team, including all team members involved (procurement or supply management, IT, any department heads) times their associated fully-burdened hourly labor cost.
- Subtract the ECE's fee (should be $0 if you are using the savings guarantee figure).
- Add the incremental results your internal team will generate with other projects during the time they are not engaged in this expense category.
- This equals your net benefit of cost savings in this expense category.

Once you have two figures to compare, ask yourself:

1. Which choice generates the highest return to my company?
2. What is my confidence level that the option with the highest return will deliver on its commitment?

You will now have your answer to who should recover the hard dollar savings for the expense category you just evaluated.

Chapter 5 Takeaways

How do you decide whether your internal team or an ECE is best suited to maximize cost savings in a particular expense category?

Compare the written commitments of your internal team and an ECE.

Compare the consequences of each for not delivering on their commitment.

Evaluate the opportunity cost of the other initiatives that your internal team could be working on if an ECE has committed to delivering at least the same hard dollar savings as your internal team.

Consider the direct industry experience of your internal team and an ECE (this is not experience buying from the industry but rather actually working within it).

Chapter Gifts

In summary, evaluate which resource will produce the best outcome. You can download a spreadsheet designed specifically for your comparison listed as resource document #7, "What's my best option? Double check comparison," at:

www.slashyouroperatingbudget.com/resources

You can download a template that will allow you to summarize your internal team's direct industry experience for the expense category you are analyzing listed as resource document #8, "My internal team industry experience checklist," at:

www.slashyouroperatingbudget.com/resources

Chapter Six

What's the Real Benefit of an Expense Category Expert (ECE)?

"There are two kinds of success. One is the very rare kind that comes to the person who has the power to do what no one else has the power to do. That is genius. But the average person who wins what we call success is not a genius. That person is a man or woman who has merely the ordinary qualities that they share with their fellows, but who has developed those ordinary qualities to a more than ordinary degree."

– Theodore Roosevelt

Let's examine client-vendor dynamics.

The client wants to receive the "best value" possible. Clients describe "best value" as their personal optimal mix of low price and best possible customer support. Because each company has its own culture and methods of operation, each company has a different perception of what "optimal" is.

Vendors want to be selected to supply you with their products and services at the highest profit level possible.

Obviously these are opposing goals. Each side compromises to a level where each feels they are satisfied with their cost and benefit. The more one side wins, the more the other side loses.

Each side usually wants to maximize their value and doesn't know how they can restructure the agreement to achieve more of what they want while giving more of something not as important to them.

Enter the ECE. While not intended to be a benefit for the vendor (although there is a vendor benefit, too... more on that in a minute), the ECE has deep insight and understanding of the vendor's world. They were working within the vendor's world at one point in their career.

How would the outcome of a football game change if one of the teams had their opponent's playbook in advance? Every time their opponent would run a play, the defensive would already know what was being done and could not only block it but set their offense up for their own optimal results.

I realize the reader could raise a question of ethics in this football example, but the ECE gained the vendor's "playbook" with years of their own personally invested experience, and you can leverage their knowledge and experience as a true advocate for your business.

Like the vendor, the ECE has a deep and thorough knowledge of the industry. Unlike the vendor, the ECE's goals are perfectly aligned with yours... to receive the best possible value from the vendor. By maximizing the value you receive from the vendor, performance (contingency) based ECEs maximize their own reward. Perfect alignment of goals.

The ECE is willing to join your team temporarily at no out-of-pocket cost to you. With no up-front cost, they leverage their industry knowledge and experience to obtain the best possible value from that industry's vendors. You select the offer or package that best meets your company's definition of best possible value.

The ECE is compensated from a portion of the savings they generated; from the budget dollars that used to be paid to the vendors.

The benefit of an ECE to any vendor (except your current, incumbent vendor) is that they get to participate in a request for proposal process that they would not be involved in otherwise. The larger companies that I work with don't change vendors very often and, as a result, are rarely open to reviewing new vendors' products or services.

The ECE's role is to thoroughly evaluate the vendor community without engaging your company's labor resources. The ECE then presents options in a summary format for you to review. From experience, all vendors besides your current one are eager to be part of the process.

Secret #3: An ECE is your secret weapon for achieving maximum value from your vendors.

Chapter 6 Takeaways

Your vendors and your company almost always have opposing goals.

Your goal is to receive the best possible value (your optimal mix of low price and best possible customer support). Vendors focus on being selected by you to provide their products or services at the highest price and profit margin possible.

An ECE's goals are aligned with yours. Their focus is to research and assemble a summary of product and vendor options that represent the best value for that specific expense category.

An ECE cannot by definition provide any of the products or services that they are researching for you. Their compensation should be based solely on the hard dollar benefit (savings) they generate for you. They should allow you to make product and vendor selections and be compensated exclusively by you.

The criteria just mentioned ensure that the ECE is working solely for your company's benefit and your mutual goals are perfectly aligned. The more you win, the more they win.

As a side note, the ECE should always benchmark current product and service quality on the front end and only provide your company with options that meet or exceed those benchmarks.

Chapter Gifts

You can download a summary of the 11 step cost reduction system that my company uses listed as resource document #9, "BottomLine Advantage's 11 step cost savings system outline," at:

www.slashyouroperatingbudget.com/resources

You can download an ECE Qualification Checklist listed as resource document #10, "ECE qualification checklist," at:

www.slashyouroperatingbudget.com/resources

Chapter Seven

How Can I Find the Right Expense Category Expert (ECE) to Help Me?

"We learn by example and by direct experience because there are real limits to the adequacy of verbal instruction."

– Malcolm Gladwell

As you've read this far, I'm assuming that you see the benefit to your company of utilizing an ECE to lower operating costs in their area of specialty.

Now the question becomes, "How do I find the right ECE for me?"

Unfortunately, this is not as easy as conducting a web search for "Expense Category Expert" which, as of this writing, yields no useful information.

Finding the first competent ECE is usually the most difficult. Once you have located, verified competency, and successfully used an ECE, they themselves can be the best source of other competent ECEs for your other key expense categories.

So how do you find the first one?

- Peer company contacts – ask if they have any experience using ECEs.
- Other professional advisors, i.e. legal, account, insurance – ask if they have any experience using ECEs.
- Industry magazines – check publication ads and even articles for a case study completed by an ECE.
- Your business mastermind group.
- Other business contacts through your industry associations or charity work.
- ECEs contacting you directly – most ECEs have an active marketing department to find new clients.

Once you locate a qualified ECE for the expense category you wish to evaluate, listed below is a checklist to help determine their fit with your needs and goals.

☐ Are they 100% performance (contingency) based with absolutely zero up-front fees? (This shifts all of the risk to the ECE.)

☐ Do they provide a written "savings *commitment*" up-front with a consequence to them if they're wrong in order to confirm the expense category is worth evaluating?

☐ Can they confirm the savings commitment with minimal current cost data to keep your time investment small until a savings guarantee is approved?

☐ Once your "savings *commitment*" is confirmed, is a written "*project savings* guarantee" provided that documents the minimum result they'll deliver? (This makes it easier to compare the ECE with internal capabilities and commitments. It also helps you decide which resource to use and identifies your return for the time your staff will invest.)

☐ Do they provide an outline of project steps with a timeline attached to each step? (You know up-front the flow of the project and how long the entire process will take.)

☐ Do you stay in control of project milestone decisions as well as the final vendor selection? (You know best what's important to your organization.)

☐ Does the ECE's executive management have "significant" industry experience? ("Significant" being defined as having been executive management for a vendor company for at least five years within their industry of expertise.)

☐ Are they an expert in a single expense category or a master of many? (Like a medical specialist, a true specialist or expert *focuses on one* expense category.)

☐ Do they pay all of their own expenses while working with your firm? (This saves you even more.)

☐ Do they belong to a consortium of other individual ECEs that utilize the same performance business model and engagement agreement? (This allows you to continue to lower costs in additional expense categories without having to review additional agreement paperwork and business processes.)

☐ Does the ECE commit up-front to making a donation to your favorite charity (in your company's name) of at least $1,000 after completing your cost savings project?

I recently did a web search for "cost reduction consultants." While it did yield more information than "ECE," it looked like the companies listed were more procurement oriented than true ECEs.

The descriptions I saw at their websites were those of professional buyers. Very different than an expert from within the industry.

Apply the above checklist to one of the professional buyer companies and you'll see the difference.

If you get stuck and can't find an ECE for a particular expense category, feel free to contact me at help@slashyouroperatingbudget.com or call 888-400-3600 extension 630. I'll check our ECE consortium for the resource you need.

Chapter 7 Takeaways

How do I find the right Expense Category Expert (ECE)?

Check the list included above for places to start looking for a competent ECE.

Once you've identified a qualified ECE candidate, use the checklist above to confirm they're a fit for your company.

Chapter Gifts

You can download a template that will outline all the criteria to make sure you have when engaging a contingency-based ECE listed as resource document #11, "Contingency checklist," at:

www.slashyouroperatingbudget.com/resources

Chapter Eight

Risk – What Could Go Wrong?

"If we allow risk to be a fear, then we are sure not to succeed. But, if we approach risk with proper planning and a good attitude, then most times we can minimize the risk and use it to our advantage."

– George S. Patton

Any business decision carries some amount of risk. Let's review what can go wrong when you engage an ECE. I'll list of all the possibilities I can come up with and, below each one, suggest ways to protect yourself.

- The ECE charges an up-front fee and either disappears without warning or ends up falling short of your expectations or their savings commitments.

  Competent ECEs should be using a performance-based business model *without any up-front fee*. They are compensated only after they deliver a result which you agreed upon up-front. The result should be clearly demonstrated and able to be confirmed by you.

- The ECE takes a lot of your staff's time and either disappears without warning or ends up falling short of your expectations or their savings commitments.

  Check the ECE's credentials up-front. Any competent ECE will have testimonials or clients that are willing to speak to you live, if requested. Ask about their industry experience and be on the lookout for any inconsistencies.

- The ECE is just a vendor disguised as a client advocate and tries to pigeonhole you into a predefined solution.

  Question your potential ECE before hiring them about the company they represent and their corporate mission statement. You're looking for any hint that they or their company is not an unbiased client advocate. If you hear any comments about pre-existing vendor and manufacturer relationships or predefined solutions, you're most likely talking with a vendor or a front company connected to a vendor.

What you are looking for is an ECE that will evaluate your specific needs and assess all qualified vendors that can serve your company. This is a thorough marketplace evaluation customized for your business.

- The ECE pressures your company to engage with a vendor that you are not comfortable using.

A competent ECE will make it clear up-front that *you* will make all decisions at project milestones and that you'll determine the vendor solution you wish to select. The ECE is a guide, like a Sherpa who knows the surrounding terrain intimately. The ECE assembles a collection of vendor options that are available only to "industry insiders," but you make all decisions regarding who you'll select to use.

- The ECE is not meeting any timelines that you have agreed to.

The agreement the ECE uses to outline their services and deliverables should contain a section listing the steps in their process and a timetable detailing when each of those steps will be completed. If the timetables are not being met, your concern should be addressed in writing to confirm the holdup is not actually on your end (as in data requested but not yet provided).

If you determine the responsibility of the timeline failure falls solely on the ECE and it is not corrected promptly, you should evoke your cancellation privilege.

Non-compliance regarding timelines is rare on the ECE's part because it is clearly in their best interest to complete the project as agreed so they can begin receiving compensation for the results they deliver to you.

- The ECE is making commitments on behalf of your firm that they are not authorized to make.

  As mentioned above, it should be clear within the ECE's agreement that all project direction and vendor selection decisions will be made by your company.

  If you document any deviation on the part of the ECE to that policy, agreement cancellation notice should be given in writing immediately.

- The ECE fails to meet or exceed their written savings guarantee.

  The ECE only earns compensation if they exceed their savings guarantee. While you do want the ECE to exceed their savings guarantee (always assuming that product and service quality is at least maintained or even improved), what is your downside if they don't?

  You get to keep all the savings generated and have no obligation to pay any project fee. Maybe not the outcome you had hoped for, but not a bad worst-case.

While researching quotes for this book, I found an alternative way to lower corporate costs on JokeDiary.com:

COST CUTTING

DUE TO THE CURRENT FINANCIAL STATUS OF THE COMPANY, ALL EMPLOYEES ARE ENCOURAGED TO ADOPT THE FOLLOWING COST CUTTING MEASURES.

Lodging

All employees are encouraged to stay with relatives and friends while on business travel. If weather permits, public areas such as parks should be used as temporary lodging sites. Bus terminals, train stations, and office lobbies may provide shelter in periods of inclement weather.

Transportation

Hitchhiking is the preferred mode of travel in lieu of commercial transport. Luminescent safety vests will be issued to all employees prior to their departure on business trips. Bus transportation will be used only when work schedules require such travel. Airline tickets will be authorized in extreme circumstances and the lowest fares will be used. For example, if a meeting is scheduled in Seattle but the lower fare can be obtained by traveling to Detroit, then travel to Detroit will be substituted for travel to Seattle.

Meals

Expenditures for meals will be limited to an absolute minimum. It should be noted that certain grocery and specialty chains such as Hickory Farms, General Nutrition centers, and Costco or Sam's stores, etc. often provide free samples of promotional items. Entire meals can be obtained in this manner. Travelers should also be familiar with indigenous roots, berries, and other protein sources available at their destinations.

If restaurants must be utilized, travelers should use "all you can eat" salad bars. This is especially effective for employees traveling together as one plate can be used to feed the entire group. Employees are also encouraged to bring their own food on business travel. Cans of tuna fish, Spam, and Beefaroni can be consumed at your leisure without the necessary bother of heating or costly preparation.

Miscellaneous

All employees are encouraged to devise innovative techniques in an effort to save company dollars. One enterprising individual has already suggested that money could be raised during airport layover periods which could be used to defray travel expenses. In support of this idea, red caps will be issued to all employees prior to their departure so that they may earn tips by helping others with their luggage. Small plastic roses and ball point pens will also be available to employees so that sales may be made as time permits.

Chapter 8 Takeaways

Since risk is a component within every business decision, what's your risk using an ECE?

Review the risk explanations listed above and let me know if you feel I've missed any at:

help@slashyouroperatingbudget.com

Chapter Nine

Can I Really "Partner" with a Vendor?

Most people are skeptical about the wrong things and gullible about the wrong things."

– Nassim Nicholas Taleb

During my 33 years of industry experience both as a vendor and an ECE, I've heard clients and prospective clients comment that they're looking for a vendor that they can "partner with."

When asked for clarification of what "partnering with their vendor" meant to them, they would say something like choosing a vendor that acts in their (the client's) best interest.

Do I think that's possible? Yes.

Do I think it's nearly impossible to pull off? Yes.

Let me explain why.

Any company, including yours, exists to earn profit by selling its products and/or services. From my experience and observation, the profit motive is strong indeed.

It makes sense because gross profit is what pays salaries, commissions, and bonuses. And those pay for lifestyle, at whatever level it is.

Partnering sounds good and, in principle, makes perfect sense. Two entities cooperating to reap benefits greater than either one could by itself is a sound notion.

I feel that with perfect transparency, vendor partnering has a chance. But "perfect transparency" to me means each entity has full knowledge of the other's true costs, selling prices, and profits.

I've never seen an arrangement that transparent. So with each step away from "perfect transparency," the opportunity for inequity in the "partnership" grows.

From my experience, every company wants to maximize their own profit. And on each side of a client-vendor equation, you have hidden information.

The client wants to buy the needed product or service at the lowest possible price while receiving the highest possible quality and customer support.

The vendor, on the other hand, wants to earn the client's business at the highest possible price while providing quality and customer support that is acceptable to the client and least costly for the vendor to provide.

These are directly opposing goals.

The client side of the partnership must be vigilant by continuously evaluating marketplace competition to compare the pricing and quality/support they receive from their "partner" with the pricing and quality/support offered by the vendor community.

Recently I was at a client's office helping them select their vendor of choice from a list of vendor finalists. These are in-person interviews with potential vendors' sales and support teams.

A Regional VP of Sales for the potential vendor commented that, because the equipment and support portion of their industry had become commoditized, they were now focused on partnering with their clients to find additional ways to provide value.

He explained the several ways they did that and the benefit to the client.

It all sounded good, but it got me thinking… isn't this a lot like keeping your attention on the area where you're used to comparing value while they are off getting better margins elsewhere within your company?

Again, if the relationship is perfectly transparent, no worries. If it isn't, make sure you aren't disclosing your current costs in the areas your "partnered vendor" is proposing improvements. If they think they can improve new areas, let the vendor propose their solution without knowing your current costs in that area.

Secret #4: Vendors will find ways to maximize their profits over time.

Do your own analysis about the real value. If you agree, then you can implement the proposed solution and only then reveal your savings to your vendor. This allows the vendor to look for additional ways to benefit your company while ensuring that you didn't overpay for their proposed solution.

In the absence of "perfect transparency," I suggest adding an expert to your team that is in complete alignment with your company's goals.

A competent ECE has a deep and intimate knowledge of the industry in which they are an expert. They've lived as a vendor and, if you've chosen the right expert, they've held a position within executive management of the industry (for at least five years).

The ECE is typically 100% performance (contingency) based and rewarded in some proportion to the amount of hard dollar savings they generate for you (while maintaining or improving quality and support provided by the vendor).

Now you have a true partner. They have a good understanding of what your goals are and they have full knowledge of the vendor's industry. They know what to ask, how to ask it, and when they've actually received the best value from the vendor community.

The better their results, the better off you are and the greater their reward. Perfect alignment of goals.

One aside. A true ECE is a master of one industry. I guess it's possible, but I've never met (or heard of) an ECE that has executive management career experience in multiple industries.

When I've seen a multi-industry expert, it always turned out that the expert has been on the buying side (procurement or supply management) of the equation, not the vendor side.

The choice is yours, but for my money, I want an expert on my team that's been inside an industry at the highest level. They know the industry's true costs, motivators, and how those motivators change throughout the calendar year.

They know how to "repackage" your account and present it to make it most attractive to that industry's vendors. As I said before, they know what to ask, how to ask it, and recognize when they've received the best possible value that vendors can provide.

Chapter 9 Takeaways

Is "partnering" with your vendor possible? Unfortunately, with opposing goals and the lack of complete transparency, partnering with you vendor is nearly impossible to truly implement.

If a vendor wants to provide your company with new options for cost reduction and/or operating efficiencies, don't provide your current costs to the vendor. Ask them for their written solutions proposal and then compare it your current costs or system.

An ECE can be helpful here by acting as a "firewall" by collecting multiple vendors' proposed solutions and leveraging their experience to summarizing the options as well as comparing them to your current costs and system. A competent ECE can "level the playing field" and allow you to easily compare different vendor solutions.

Chapter Ten

Two Emotions That are Costing You Hundreds of Thousands to Millions in Profits….

"Minds are like parachutes. They only function when they are open."

– James Dewar

I've already mentioned some of the many versions of the following objections to having an ECE "double check" (meaning review your current costs in order to estimate your hard dollar savings potential) and only one is truly legitimate. Although a strong statement, stay with me and I'll explain why.

Skepticism

Skepticism is our natural reaction to having been taken advantage of or deceived in the past. The next time anything looks similar to what tricked us before, our internal red flags pop up to either avoid the request, offer, or situation or slow it down enough so we can thoroughly evaluate. Most of the time we avoid it. Skepticism is a good response... if you take one more next step.

If you've ever watched American Greed, you have seen firsthand the seemingly endless ways that you can be "taken." It's no wonder that skepticism is alive and well.

The problem is that skepticism also blocks opportunities as it builds its wall of protection.

Your solution is to let skepticism motivate you to question an ECE's claims of being able to produce significant cost savings. A competent ECE should be able to estimate your savings potential up-front as well as the time needed from your team so you can decide if it's worth your time.

Evaluating Your Risk

- Is there any up-front fee?
- Have I been given a savings potential estimate (better yet, a savings potential guarantee!)?
- How much of my time (or my organization's time) is needed to confirm the savings potential?

- Once the savings potential is confirmed by the ECE, has a project savings guarantee been provided?
- How much of my team's time will the entire process take?
- Who else has the ECE successfully generated hard dollar cost savings for?

Your total risk should be limited to the time your team invests providing the ECE with current cost data. With reasonably organized data, that should be about an hour or less of labor time to confirm savings potential.

Once savings potential is confirmed, a competent ECE will provide you with a written guarantee to outline your worst case outcome (and the ECE assuming all the risk of performance).

Remember – the ECE has incentive to surpass their guarantee.

If your risk is higher than that, I think you're talking with the wrong ECE.

Fear

Fear is typically even more deeply rooted and is less rational than skepticism. It comes from negative experiences with a similar event or fearing an unwanted outcome from an event. From personal experience with prospective clients and clients exhibiting fear symptoms, I've learned that fearful individuals project catastrophic outcomes happening to them.

After several successful cost reduction projects, my primary contacts (usually in procurement or supply management) confided to me that on the front end of the project they saw themselves being chastised by their bosses because someone other than them (our company) found significant hard dollar savings while they were managing the expense category.

They further projected that that they would lose their job as a result of the savings recovery and upon telling their spouse, the spouse would leave their marriage. This broke up their family and they visualized themselves being broken and devastated.

Wow! All this from helping their company achieve cost savings!

After hearing this several times from reluctant client team members (only after successfully recovering several hundred thousand hard dollars each time), I realized how real and deeply rooted this fear is.

I'm not making fun of people with these fears as I struggle with my own irrational fear (roller coasters). I know from experience that fear makes you feel as if death is approaching.

During the eight years I've been serving as an ECE and a business owner in my industry, I've not seen or developed a way to help client team members face this fear. It's only after we've successfully recovered hard dollar savings that they breathed a sigh of relief. They realized that their executive management was happy to have recovered additional operating capital and were not going to punish or fire them.

My advice to executive management is:

Give your procurement or supply management staff "permission" (make it explicitly clear it's OK to use outside ECEs) to accomplish exceptional cost savings using whatever expertise they can assemble.

Of course, your permission is given with the condition that any ECEs engaged are 100% performance (contingency) based with absolutely zero up-front fees and provide at least a written project savings guarantee (so there's no out-of-pocket cost and you know where you'll end up, worst case, before your start).

You can copy the ECE qualifications check list provided in Chapter Seven or go to:

www.slashyouroperatingbudget.com/resources and select resource document #10 listed as, "ECE qualification checklist," to download a copy for your team.

Use the permission form on the next page to confirm for your team that it's okay to explore outside cost savings opportunities.

Secret #5: Skepticism and fear are costing your company hundreds to thousands to millions in profits.

"No pessimist ever discovered the secrets of the stars, or sailed to an uncharted land, or opened a new heaven to the human spirit."

– Helen Keller

Permission Form to Explore Saving Opportunities

_____ (Team Member Name) is hereby given permission to explore hard dollar cost savings opportunities for _____ (Company Name).

Leveraging external Expense Category Experts may be evaluated and implemented without fear of it reflecting poorly on your professional skill or expertise.

Similar to the medical industry's hierarchy of specialists, it is understood that no one person has comprehensive knowledge of all expense categories.

Our desired goal is to lower hard dollar operating costs while maintaining the same or better quality of product/service and vendor support.

_____

Executive Approval

_____

Executive's Printed Name

_____

Title

_____

Date

Timing

The only objection I've ever found to be legitimate is one related to "timing." Timing is defined here as new agreements having recently been put in place within a specific expense category that prevent any changes at the current time. This doesn't mean the best agreement is in place, it simply means changes can't be made until later in the current agreement or at its expiration date.

And this is only an issue if the recent agreement encompasses all the equipment, products, or services that a vendor provides to you. If you have other agreements expiring over time, you can implement a cost reduction review at any time.

If you confirm that an expense category review is not possible now, when the timing is right, be sure to have an ECE double check your current agreements (at no charge, of course). This ensures you're operating as efficiently as possible (always measured from the perspective of *your* best mix of lowest cost and best possible vendor support and performance).

I hope this guide has helped you look at your operating cost evaluation practices in a new light. While the traditional "get at least three bids" approach is somewhat effective, I advise any company to do their own due diligence and get a no-cost and risk-free double check on their current methods and results. I know you'll be pleasantly surprised and glad you did!

Chapter 10 Takeaways

Two emotions that are costing your firm from hundreds of thousands to millions in profits... skepticism and fear.

While working together, Ray Seabrook, then-CFO of Ball Corporation (301 on the 2013 Fortune 500 list at $8.7 billion in annual revenues) said, "we focus mostly on our core expenses but if you never look at the other 80%, they'll eat your lunch."

Evaluate your risk rather than allowing skepticism to stifle your opportunity to return wasted hard dollars to your operating budget and/or bottom line.

Use the checklist provided above or any other tool you've developed to evaluate risk.

Using a competent ECE, there's never an up-front cost, you get a double check for free, and when they successfully recover hard dollars from your operating budget, you'll pay them with funds previously being overpaid to one of your vendors.

Regarding wasting time (false promises), a competent ECE will provide a roadmap and outcome guarantees up-front. Their process should be broken down into steps so you can unplug the project before investing much time. The ECE's guarantees should include a consequence to them for being wrong. With this type of risk reversal, the ECE clearly has the biggest risk for non-performance.

Fear is the tougher emotion to manage. Because it triggers negative sub-conscious panic, rarely can it be "talked through." The most effective remedy I've seen is for executives (who are rarely involved in vendor management) to give permission to the expense category manager to reduce costs using any ethical and corporate culture approved methods they have available. This includes using outsourced expense category experts (ECEs).

The permission form is listed above and can also be downloaded at: www.slashyouroperatingbudget.com/resources and is labeled as resource document #12, "Savings permission form."

Although giving permission may seem unneeded and silly, I can assure you that the emotion of fear has prevented numerous companies from enjoying significantly lower (as in hundreds of thousands to millions of hard dollars) operating costs because the expense category managers are deathly afraid of the consequences of any semblance of incompetence. It's often been shared with me that bringing in outside help gives the impression of weakness and/or a lack of skill.

Although the medical profession has long enjoyed the benefits of leveraging specialized training and experience, the business sector has yet to embrace this concept.

Business executives can take a simple step to minimize this irrational fear of repercussions resulting from outsourcing to niche experts. Your company can achieve exceptional results on a risk-free basis by simply giving permission to their expense category managers to explore all avenues to meet or exceed targeted objectives.

If you have any questions about the information contained in this book or you need help in a specific expense category, you're welcome to e-mail your question to:

help@slashyouroperatingbudget.com

or call 888.400.3600 extension 630.

Although my company is an expert in one expense category, we have formed a consortium of other niche expense category experts that operate in the identical, risk-free, no up-front cost and guaranteed results manner. I am happy to answer your questions or introduce you to an ECE that can assist within a specific expense category. You can contact me via this book's e-mail address:

help@slashyouroperatingbudget.com

or call 888-400-3600 extension 630.

Chapter Gifts

You can download the digital version of the permission form printed above which is listed as resource document #12, "Savings permission form," at:

www.slashyouroperatingbudget.com/resources

Resources

Listed below are templates that can be downloaded at www.slashyouroperatingbudget.com. They were created to help you double check your company's expense categories and cost monitoring systems from a new perspective.

Use the templates to test whether your company has a cost savings potential of at least $227,325 (like 89% of the companies we review).

Doc #	Resource Document Description	Chapter Reference
1	The hard dollar value of my internal team's cost reduction targets	1
2	Savings potential checklist	1
3	Budget stalled initiatives	2
4	When were our expense categories last reviewed? -lists all major expense categories	2
5	Savings Commitment template	3
6	Project Savings Guarantee	4
7	What's my best option? - double check comparison	5
8	My internal team industry experience checklist	5
9	BottomLine Advantage's 11 step cost savings system outline	6
10	ECE qualification checklist	6
11	Contingency checklist	7
12	Savings permission form	10

Notes

Notes

Notes

_____

_____

_____

_____

_____

_____

_____

_____

_____

_____

_____

_____

_____

_____

_____

_____

_____

_____

_____

_____

_____

_____

_____

_____

_____

_____

Notes

Notes

Notes

Notes

Notes

Notes

Notes

Notes

Notes

About The Author

After graduating from North Carolina State University and experiencing Maui Hawaii's beauty for two years, David Cantliffe moved to Boulder, Colorado in 1979 to attend the University of Colorado's MBA program. During his first spring semester, he decided to get some business to business selling experience and joined a locally owned copier distributor.

David's copy, fax, and print experience in a vendor role spans over 23 years of serving customers in the Denver metropolitan area as well as customer locations throughout the entire nation.

Working within an independent distributorship, the multinational and multi-billion dollar IKON (now known as Ricoh USA), as well as co-founding an independent dealership have given David a complete understanding of vendors' business models.

BottomLine Advantage LLC was founded in 2005 to serve as an advocate for companies that demand their operating budgets run as lean as possible. David leveraged his 23+ year vendor experience to design a market and vendor evaluation system which yields the highest possible value from your selected vendor. This system contradicts the "common wisdom" that low price also means low quality. BottomLine Advantage LLC consistently over-delivers on its written performance guarantees that encompass hard dollar cost reduction, equipment performance, and vendor support metrics.

At the time of this writing, BottomLine Advantage has recovered and returned over $15.9 million hard dollars for clients while simultaneously maintaining or enhancing all benchmarked equipment and vendor support metrics.

David coined the term "Expense Category Expert" to describe expense category niche experts. Like the medical profession's specialization, Expense Category Experts (ECEs) produce an exceptional result in their respective niche specialty.

After being asked numerous times to assist with cost reduction and vendor support enhancements within other expense categories, David saw the need to assemble other niche experts willing to help clients using the same performance based, deliver results first business model. Nicknamed "The Consortium," the member ECE's have the skill and experience to implement market and vendor evaluations for all major expense categories without any up-front costs to clients.

Questions? You may reach David by e-mail at:

help@slashyouroperatingbudget.com

or by calling 888-400-3600 extension 630.

www.ingramcontent.com/pod-product-compliance
Lightning Source LLC
Chambersburg PA
CBHW071528200326
41519CB00019B/6115